A Catechist's PRAYER Companion

Personal Prayers That Encourage & Guide

KATHLEEN GLAVICH, SND

twentythirdpublications.com

*To catechists worldwide,
especially Catherine Miles-Flynn
and Joseph Flynn,
who for years have helped to ensure that
the Good News of Jesus Christ
is heard in Arabia.*

TWENTY-THIRD PUBLICATIONS
977 Hartford Turnpike Unit A; Waterford, CT 06385
(860) 437-3012 or (800) 321-0411 • www.twentythirdpublications.com

Copyright © 2023 Kathleen Glavich, SND. All rights reserved.
No part of this publication may be reproduced in any manner without prior written permission of the publisher. Write to the Permissions Editor.

IMAGE CREDITS: Cover photo: stock.adobe.com/busra; Interior: stock.adobe.com

ISBN: 978-1-62785-777-2 • Printed in the U.S.A.

One day, in the quiet cave of your heart,
you heard God whisper, "Go into all the world
and proclaim the Good News."
He called you as surely as he called
Peter, James, John, and the other apostles.

So now you are God's catechist,
handpicked to form God's young disciples.
Let God's love shine through you to them.

Enter your classroom
with courage and determination.
Plant the seeds of faith
that will take root,
grow strong,
and spread.

You are not alone as you perform
the spiritual work of mercy "instruct the ignorant."
Jesus promised, "I am with you."
His Holy Spirit empowers you
to carry out your vital mission
for the Church today and for its future.

Your sisters and brothers in the Church
thank you for your work of evangelizing.
May you be blessed for saying yes,
and may you be a blessing to others.

Prayers for Myself as a Catechist	Prayers for My Ministry	Prayers to My Special Aides	Prayers for Holidays, Holy Days, and Seasons
page 4	page 20	page 38	page 42

PRAYERS FOR
Myself as a Catechist

Prayer to Strengthen My Bond with Jesus

Jesus, by my baptism I was consecrated to you.
Over the years I learned about you
    in Scripture and through what others told me.
I am attracted to your goodness,
    your wisdom, and your boundless mercy.

I can hardly believe
    that you, the mighty Son of God,
    despite the immense chasm between
    divinity and humanness,
    became human
    and died for my sake.
How amazing that you love me that much
    and, what's more, desire my love!

As my knowledge of you has grown,
    so has my love for you.
Speaking with you in prayer—
    alone and with the community of believers—
    and especially receiving you in the Eucharist
    have brought me closer to you.

Now that I am a catechist,
    I want our personal relationship
    to become stronger and more intimate.
When my love for you burns brightly,
    my students will be more likely
    to catch fire, too, and
    become your fervent disciples.

Keep me near to your heart, Jesus,
 my God, my Savior, my Love. *Amen.*

Prayer to Deepen My Prayer Life

Jesus, I know that prayer is the key
 to a blessed life on Earth
 and a happy eternity.
You stressed the importance of prayer
 by preaching about it
 and by praying often,
 in various places and at different times.

So, I ask, like a disciple did,
 "Teach me to pray."
I often pray rote prayers,
 but I would like to expand my repertoire.
Help me to experiment with other forms of prayer,
 such as meditation, mantras, *lectio divina*,
 centering prayer, and journaling.

Teach me the art of quietly listening to you.
Remind me of your presence during the day,
 prompting me to send you brief messages
 of adoration, thanksgiving, and love.

I want to make prayer a priority
 and to reserve time for it no matter
 how many activities crowd my day.

The more I keep in touch with you,
 the more I will be able to convey your Good News
 and reflect your love to my students
 in a credible and convincing way. *Amen.*

Prayer of Gratitude for My Call

Jesus, I am proud to be a catechist,
 a special way of being a missionary disciple.
I join a long parade of catechists who have
 resounded the story of your saving acts
 over some two thousand years.
You called twelve apostles to continue your ministry
 of proclaiming the kingdom of God,
and now you have called me
 to be your hands and feet and voice.

When Saint Paul listed church ministers*
 he gave teachers a place of honor:
 right after apostles and prophets.
To him my ministry outweighed performing miracles,
 healing, and speaking in tongues.

Thank you for choosing me for this gift of teaching.
Thank you for this opportunity to carry on
 your prophetic mission
 that I inherited at my baptism.
Not only am I privileged
 to pass on the treasure of our faith to others,
 to share what I have been given,
 but as I do so,
 my own faith will be nurtured.

Thank you for the catechists and everyone else
 who taught me the faith.
Thank you for the knowledge, experience, and grace
 you provided to prepare me
 for this church ministry.

May I live up to the confidence you place in me.
I know you are counting on me
    to echo the Gospel for a new generation. *Amen.*

*1 Corinthians 12:28

Prayer to Be a Good Catechist

Jesus, with all my heart I desire
    to be a good catechist.

Help me to teach with love for all my students
    so that they come to know
    your love for them.
    Let me see you in them.

Help me to understand the great truths
    of our faith and take steps to learn
        more about them.

Help me to deliver my lessons wisely and clearly
    with conviction and even passion,
    enabling my students to cultivate
    a lifelong friendship with you.

Help me to employ a variety of methods
    to reach students of every learning style
    and keep them engaged.

Help me to be open to the inspiration
    of the Holy Spirit as I plan and as I teach.
    Make me willing to try new things.

Help me to grow in faith, hope, and love
    so that all my words and actions
    are a bridge to you,
    who are our way, truth, and life.

Help me to be a faithful witness to you
    and to model Gospel living
    so that my students will be inspired,
    yes, compelled, to follow you.

Help me to proclaim the Good News
    of salvation with joy and good humor
    so that my classroom rings with laughter.

I trust that after I've been your good servant,
    I will reap the reward you promised:
        those who teach will shine like stars
        for all eternity.* *Amen.*

*Daniel 12:3

Prayer to the Divine Teacher

Jesus, in the Gospels, people most often
    called you "teacher."
I wish to be a teacher like you.
Please be my mentor.

It didn't matter
if you had one student like Nicodemus
    or five thousand,
if your setting was a hillside
    or a boat on the Sea of Galilee,
if people soaked in your words like Mary of Bethany
    or if they argued with you like the Scribes and Pharisees,
    or if they walked away.
You always gave your all.

May I always give my all, too,
    no matter how many students are in my class,
    no matter the space where I teach,
    no matter how my teaching is received.

You taught by stories and pithy sayings.
Lacking textbooks, technology, and modern audiovisuals,
 you used the natural world around you:
 sparrows, flowers, seeds, water, fire.
You shaped your message to your listeners
 whether they were farmers or fishermen,
 young children or wise men in the Temple.

Help me to deliver your word
 whatever my tools and supplies
 in ways that appeal to my students
 and touch their hearts.

Your most memorable lessons were your acts of love:
 praying all night, healing lepers, washing feet,
 and, above all, sacrificing your life.

People were amazed at your teaching.
I can't hope to amaze my students.
But with your grace I can bring them closer to God
 and the kingdom of God,
 especially by the witness of my love. *Amen.*

Prayer to Grow in Understanding Scripture

Jesus, thank you for the gift of Sacred Scripture
 that reveals our Triune God:
 Creator, Savior, and Holy Spirit.
In it you unfold mysteries of life,
 recount the history of God's dealings with humanity,
 and, above all, declare your love for us.

I want to delve into the riches of
 the Scripture verses,
 for they deepen my knowledge of you.

Prompt me to take courses on the Bible,
> read commentaries on it,
> pay attention to homilies flowing from it,
> and ponder your divine words.

I believe that in the Bible you speak to us.
Give me ears to hear your words
> and a heart to understand them.

Let me use Scripture as the grist of my prayer,
> attuned to personal messages you send me.

Because the Bible is the wellspring of our faith
along with Tradition,
> I ask you to inspire me with ways
> to acquaint my students with it.

Help me to weave verses through my lessons,
> assign passages to memorize,
> and teach how to pray with Scripture.

Make me a fitting instrument
> to communicate and interpret your sacred words.

May my students not only become familiar
> with your Holy Bible
> but make reading it a habit
> and grow to love it. *Amen.*

Prayer to Increase My Love for the Eucharist

Jesus, what a tremendous gift
> you gave us in the Eucharist!

When we gather around your table
as your Church, your holy people,
> we participate in your redemption.
> Your sacrifice becomes our sacrifice.

And we also offer ourselves to the Father.

At Mass we praise and thank the Father
in the most excellent way
    and in the company of the saints and angels.
The liturgy teaches us the mysteries of faith.

What's more astonishing,
we can consume you
    body and blood, soul, and divinity.
We become one with you
    and with one another.

May I never take this queen of the sacraments
    for granted.
Let me celebrate each Eucharist
    with as much love and devotion
    as though it were my last one.

May my deep love of the Eucharist
impact my students
    so that they, too, cherish it
    and take every opportunity
    to celebrate it.

I look forward to your eternal banquet,
where we will offer praise and thanks
    forever. *Amen.*

Prayer for Wisdom

Jesus, like Solomon I ask for the gift of wisdom:
    not for reigning over a kingdom
    but for leading the miniature Church,
    the students in my class.

Grant me the wisdom…

to answer students' questions correctly
    and promise to find out answers I don't know,
  to acknowledge that I am not always right,
  to identify the students who need extra praise,
  to shape the lessons to my students' ability,
  to sense how the students are feeling,
  to take into account factors outside the classroom
    that might be impacting my students,
  to change a lesson mid-stream if necessary,
  to avoid judging students unfairly,
  to keep my personal problems and concerns
    from affecting my teaching,
  to realize that every lesson will not be perfect,
  to ask for help when I need it,
  to rely on you and your grace for success,
  to desire not to be popular but rather
    to be respected and remembered by the students
    as someone who made them love you more.

Hear my prayer, Jesus,
and I will be an effective catechist,
  an icon of you,
  and a spiritual companion who influences my students
  to embrace Christian living.
That way they will enjoy abundant life
  in this world and in the one on the horizon. *Amen.*

Prayer for Patience

Jesus, you exercised patience many times:
  when the Scribes and Pharisees
    antagonized you,
  when the apostles failed to understand
    your teaching,

when people resisted your news
    about the bread of life
    and abandoned you.
Even now you are patient with me
    when I cling to sins and bad habits!

Help me to be patient with students
    who need more time,
    who are uncooperative,
    who don't do their homework,
    who come late,
    who misbehave,
    who break and spill things.

Help me to be patient with parents
    who complain about me or the class,
    who don't abide by our policies,
    who fail to nurture their child's faith.

Help me to be patient with myself
    when my lesson doesn't go well,
    when my unkindness hurts a student,
    when I am in a bad mood,
    when I am tired,
    when I do something embarrassing.

Help me to remain closely united to you, Jesus,
    like a branch on a vine
    so that I bear this fruit of the Holy Spirit:
    patience. *Amen.*

Prayer for Courage to Keep On

Jesus, I began this school year
with the anticipation and enthusiasm
    of a child looking forward to a birthday.

I was eager to help young people to
    encounter you and become
    knowledgeable and faith-filled Catholics.
Now my zeal has evaporated,
    and my energy has drained away.
I feel like quitting.
There are several reasons for this.

Some of my students are a handful,
    testing me, challenging me,
    and disobeying me.
They come to class angry, apathetic,
    and ready to reject or ignore
    what I say.
I might as well be talking to stones.

I'm discouraged when I learn
    that my students may have
    damaged equipment or furniture
    in the classroom.

I doubt that I have the background
    needed to teach religion well.
There is so much I don't know
    about church teachings,
    church history,
    Scripture, and morality.

Besides, I find the discipline
    of preparing lessons
    and coming to class each week
    is wearing me down.

But I don't want to be a quitter.
There is too much at stake.

So, Jesus, make me stouthearted.
Give me the courage
   to fulfill my commitment to the great,
   all-important work of catechizing—
   at least for this year.

I offer my trials and frustration to you.
Use them for the good of my students. *Amen.*

Prayer for When I'm Too Busy to Prepare

Jesus, some weeks I feel
   like I'm running a marathon each day.
There are doctor's appointments,
   work responsibilities,
   household chores,
   meals to shop for and prepare,
   events to go to or host,
   plus a few unexpected,
   time-consuming tasks.

Of course, I know how crucial it is
   to have a well-planned lesson.
Trying to wing it is risky and irresponsible.
I sincerely wish to be true to
   my commitment to serve you
   as a catechist.
Help me to spend a little time each day
   thinking about the next lesson.
Keep me from the temptation
   to procrastinate.

Don't let me rationalize that I can
   always show a DVD or YouTube video
   or have the students read something.

Soothing my conscience by promising
 that next week will be better
 just won't do.
Those souls in my class depend on me.
The Church depends on me.
You depend on me, Jesus.

When I'm overwhelmed with
 obligations,
please work a minor miracle and
 stretch time for me. *Amen.*

Prayer for When I Don't Feel Successful

Jesus, it could be that when you called me
 to be a catechist,
 you picked the wrong person.

I try so hard, but I see few results.
While I want my students to respond
 to lessons with glowing eyes
 and eager participation,
 too many of them seem apathetic.

Attendance is spotty.
Activities like soccer games
 and cheerleading practice
 tend to win out over religion class.

Seldom do I see my students
 or their parents at Sunday Mass.
Despite my urging love for one another,
 I catch my students
 stealing, lying, bullying, and fighting.
I lose heart and say to myself, "What's the use?"

But then I remember your disappointments,
> dare I say failures,
> as you taught.
James and John argued over
> who would be greater.
The rich young man could not give up
> his possessions to follow you.
Scribes and Pharisees turned a deaf ear
> to your teachings.

My hope is that
> my dedication and perseverance
> are bringing about a change
> in my students and in me.
I realize that I may discover
> some positive outcomes
> only in heaven.

Please give me an inkling that
somehow I am making a difference. *Amen.*

Prayer for When I Don't Feel Appreciated

Jesus, it hurts not to be thanked.
You know the feeling.
> Only one out of ten lepers
> thanked you for curing him.
I wish that as I work hard
> to present good lessons
> and devote time
to teach what sometimes
> is a difficult class,
people would show more appreciation.
It seems like I'm taken for granted.

I would love if sometime
the director of religious education
   or principal
   would pat me on the back
   and say, "Nice work,"
and if parents would tell me
in a note or in person
   that they appreciate
   what I'm doing for their child.
How happy it would make me
if a student or two or three
   would say, "Thank you,"
   or comment, "I liked that lesson,"
   as they left the room!

To be honest, at times I am thanked.
But most days I need to be content
knowing that you, Jesus,
   appreciate my efforts.
That, more than anything,
   is important to me
   and warms my heart.
So, I will go on in sheer faith,
   trusting that the Spirit
   is working through me
   and in the hearts of my students. *Amen.*

Prayer for When I Need Help

Jesus, you know how I like
    to be independent,
    to have everything under control,
    including a group of young people.
But sometimes I could use assistance.

You were not above seeking help.
When the multitude was hungry,
    you turned to your apostles to find food.
After you provided bread and fish,
    you depended on the apostles to distribute
    the meal and collect the leftovers.
On the way to Calvary, you didn't argue
    when Simon helped you carry the cross.

Several potential assistants are available to me.
    The director of religious education or school principal
        would be glad to help me,
        for instance, with discipline problems.
        Aiding us is in their job description!
    My fellow catechists can be depended on
        to supply me with ideas and moral support.
    Parents are usually happy to help out
        with school projects.
    A guest speaker or a panel could
        make my lesson more impressive
        and engaging.

Open my eyes to know when I could use help
    and the best person to enlist.
Then give me the humility to ask for assistance. *Amen.*

PRAYERS FOR
My Ministry

Prayer at the Beginning of the School Year

Jesus, this new year of teaching religion
    stretches before me like uncharted territory.

I am excited about embarking
    on this adventure of sharing
    the stories of God's goodness
    and inexhaustible love
    with a new generation.

I look forward to meeting my students.
Please prepare their hearts
    to be receptive to my lessons.
May they come to know and love you
    as I do.
May I help to form them into Christians
determined to work for peace and justice
    with a heart for all humanity.

The path ahead of me will be marked by
    joys and sorrows,
    successes and failures,
    pleasant surprises as well as adversities.
I offer you these months of religion classes,
    whatever they hold.

I trust that I will be up to any challenge
    because you will be at my side
    every step of the way.

Bless me and my students so that we
    enjoy being companions on the journey
    as we make our way to you together. *Amen.*

Prayer before Preparing a Lesson

Jesus, thank you for a manual
    that provides the lattice for my lesson.
Now enlighten me with creative ways
    to tailor this week's given plan
    to my students.

Inspire me to make the lesson
relevant and appealing
    for young people who are enthralled
    by cellphones and video games.
Make me aware of my students' needs,
    and give me the wisdom
    to know how to meet them.

Help me to keep in mind that covering
    the entire curriculum or
    having students parrot back answers
are not as important
    as setting their hearts
    on fire with love for the faith
    and love for you.

Bless my planning, and bless me
    and your young apprentices in the faith
    as my lesson unfolds,
    hopefully like a beautiful tapestry. *Amen.*

Prayer before a Class

Jesus, I am on the brink
    of teaching another lesson.
As I enter the room,
    keep me mindful
    that it is holy ground.
You will be present
as I share with my students
    the eternal truths of our faith
    and invite them to deepen
    their personal relationship with you.

May they welcome the knowledge
I intend to impart to them
    so that faith, hope,
    and love for you and others
    will always blossom in their hearts.

May all my words and actions
during this class
    be marked by reverence,
    convey your love,
    and give you greater
    honor and glory. *Amen.*

Prayer after a Class

Well, Jesus, I tried.
As usual, some students were eager to learn
    and cooperative,
        while others were lethargic.
Those who resented having to be here
    were as annoying as a toothache.

As I review how the lesson went,
give me the insight to realize
    what worked and what didn't work
    in sharing our Christian heritage
    and things of God
    with my class.
Thank you for my little successes
    when I had the students' rapt attention
    and they understood what I taught.
Let me learn from my failures, as
    when the students were bored or puzzled
    or when I showed frustration or anger
    rather than patience and love.
I want to improve.

May I always strive to do my best
    for the sake of my students,
    whom you love. *Amen.*

Prayer for My Students

Jesus, from all eternity you destined
these students to be in my care:
    the keen ones and those who are not so keen,
    the energetic ones and the quiet ones,
    the neat ones and the messy ones,
    the cheerful ones and the grumpy ones,
    the shrinking violets and the class clowns.
You trust me to hand on to all of them
    the precious truths and traditions of our faith.

Give my students ears and hearts open
    to the knowledge of God
    and our Catholic faith's great mysteries
    that will give meaning to their lives.

Help them to realize that faith
    and belonging to the Church are worthwhile.
Let them absorb Gospel values
    and be living signs of the Beatitudes.

May what I say and do
    lead them to understand
    the love you have for them
    and enkindle in them a love for you
    and your Church.

They are like soft clay in your hands, dear Potter.
Let me help you to shape them into
    zealous disciples who live by your teachings;
    witness to others in our secular, materialistic society;
    and promote God's kingdom
        of justice, peace, and love on Earth.
With your grace, may my students
    become saints. *Amen.*

Prayer for Students with Varied Learning Styles

Jesus, not all my students
    are academically inclined.
A few of them struggle to learn in traditional ways.
They look at me with blank faces
    or they fiddle with a pencil.
Seldom do they raise their hand
    to answer a question.

You treasure these students
who learn differently.
They have their own gifts
    that, with your help, I can
    guide them to discover.

They, too, are saints in the making.
Saint Thomas Aquinas was intellectually brilliant,
but Saint Joseph of Cupertino,
   who took more time to learn,
   needed a miracle to be ordained.

Help me to involve
all my students in the lessons.
I could ask some students to do tasks
   that use different skills,
   like passing out materials
   and keeping score in games.
I could call on them to answer
   questions suited to their learning style
and resist relying on
   certain students
   for quick and correct responses.

May I never embarrass any of my students
   or make them feel like failures.
I want all of them to be happy
   to be in my class
   and happy to learn more about you
   and your life-giving plan for them. *Amen.*

Prayer for Students with Special Needs

Jesus, you devoted a great deal of time
to ministering to people with disabilities:
   the blind, the deaf, the mute, the lame,
   lepers, and the possessed.
   You healed them.

As much as I would like to,
I cannot heal my students with special needs:

the girl with hearing loss,
the student who has cerebral palsy,
the boy with ADHD who can't sit still.

They are your beloved children,
made in your image.
You want them to have faith,
a good and meaningful life,
and happiness.

In various ways, I can ensure that
these young disciples learn about you
like the other students do.
Don't let me resent the extra
time and effort required
to accommodate them so
they can actively participate in class.
Help me to recognize their talents and abilities
and call attention to them.

Make me open to the courage and perseverance
these students can teach me
and their classmates.
May their presence make us more aware
of the diversity in God's people.
May it lead us to reflect on suffering
and the mystery of the cross.
Inspire me with ways to be
caring and supportive of these
gifts in my class
and of their parents.
Above all, help me to convey
your great love for them—
and my love too. *Amen.*

Prayer for a Disruptive Student

Jesus, you know how that one student
   drives me crazy.
I pour so much time and effort
   into crafting a perfect lesson,
   only to see it spoiled by that imp.

Talking out loud, making strange noises,
   passing notes, pestering other students,
     disregarding instructions, scribbling on the textbook,
   making the class laugh…
I wish I didn't have to deal with these antics.

Yes, I know bad behavior may be caused by
   poor home training,
   a psychological or physical disorder,
   a divorce,
   a desire for attention,
   or a lack of self-confidence.
Still, I'd like it to stop for everyone's sake,
   including yours!

I've tried the usual strategies
for dealing with a disruptive child:
   giving private pep talks,
   enlisting the parents' help,
   sending the student to the office.
These haven't worked.

So, now I appeal to you, Jesus.
I place this student in your hands.
   You who calmed storms and cast out demons
   surely can subdue this student
   so that I can deliver your Good News in peace.

In the meantime, help me
>   to look on this student with your eyes—
>   not with dislike but with love and compassion.
And give me patience, a ton of it! *Amen.*

Prayer for Good Discipline

Jesus, help me to establish good discipline,
>   the key to effective teaching.
I aim to create a comfortable order
so that the truths I teach will sink easily
>   into the minds and hearts
>   of my young disciples.

Give me the sense to dress appropriately
>   so that I communicate
>   the importance of religion class
>   and show respect for myself,
>   my students, and my role.

Help me achieve a peaceful atmosphere
>   by radiating confidence,
>   setting a few practical rules,
>   and acting with tender tenacity.
May I find the balance between
>   strictness and permissiveness.

My students are not angels.
Give me the wisdom to know
>   when to correct misbehavior
>   and when to overlook it.
Let me be fair in giving reprimands
>   and discipline.
Keep me from showing favoritism.

Give me the strength to act
   with self-control and dignity
   when I may be seething inside.
If I overreact, give me the grace
   to apologize.

As I counsel repeat offenders,
   inspire me with the right words
   to change their behavior.
Remind me that you live in them
   and that the most difficult students
   most need love and compassion.
Their acting out may be a defense mechanism.
Help me to forgive them.

As I maintain classroom discipline,
   let me not forget to grow in self-discipline. *Amen.*

Prayer for My Students' Parents

Jesus, parents (in some cases, grandparents)
   are children's first catechists.
They are primarily responsible
   for teaching their children
   what it means to be a Christian.
I am their collaborator, their assistant.
Ordinarily, moms and dads are the first
   to introduce their children to God,
   their loving Father who created them
   and the fascinating world around them.
Parents teach them to make the Sign of the Cross
   and pray the Hail Mary,
      to tell right from wrong,
      to share their things,
      and to love others.

Instill in the parents of my students
   the desire to raise their children
   to become ardent followers of you.
Give them the grace to set good examples.
Let them show their children
   that they value prayer
   by praying at home and going to church.
Help parents offer loving service to others,
   like their neighbors, the sick, and the poor.
Plant in them the curiosity
   to learn more about the faith themselves.

Also, Jesus, inspire me with ways
   to support the parents of my students.
Then give me the will
   to put these ideas into practice. *Amen.*

Prayer for My Colleagues

Jesus, bless those dedicated people
who work alongside me
   in teaching others about you:
      our director of religious education
      or principal, my fellow catechists,
      our secretary, our aides, and parish clergy.

Keep them mindful of the importance
   of their ministry.
They are participating
   in the salvation of the world with you.
They are guiding students to heaven
   and making Earth a kinder, more humane,
   and more peaceful place.

When their ministry becomes difficult,
    give them courage and patience.
Inspire us to support one another
    by a helping hand,
    a bit of advice,
    an encouraging word,
    a smile.

Give my colleagues the satisfaction
and the joy of knowing
    that they are pleasing you,
    enriching others' lives,
    and becoming better candidates
    for heaven themselves. *Amen.*

Prayer after a Great Lesson

Jesus, thank you so much
    for the wonderful lesson today.
My students were really with me.
No one was fooling around.
Most of them participated
    in the discussion
    and raised their hands
    to answer questions.
They even remembered
    what I taught in the last lesson!
As we prayed, the class
    was still and quiet
    and seemed focused on you.

I know this rare success
    was not all due to me.

You were there behind the scenes,
    inspiring and coaching me
    and opening the minds
    and hearts of the students.
I hope and pray that this is only one
of many outstanding lessons
    in my laboratory of faith. *Amen.*

Prayer after a Disappointing Lesson

Well, Jesus, this lesson fell flat.
Some students were in a daze.
Others were restless.
I doubt that much of what I tried to teach
    was absorbed.
For me this was a lesson in humility!

Maybe I didn't prepare well enough.
Maybe I wasn't in tune with
    how my students were feeling.
Maybe the weather affected them.
Whatever the reason,
I'm sorry.

May this failure spur me on
to spend more time preparing a lively lesson
    that captivates the students.
And may my zest in delivering
your Good News
and my evident love for you
    attract their attention
    like a magnet. *Amen.*

Prayer before Being Observed

Jesus, you know how I am a bundle of nerves
   when someone comes to watch me teach.
Calm me down and let me welcome
   this observation as a learning experience.

I realize that this visitor only means
   to help me hone my skills as a catechist.
Make me teach well this day
   and let my students behave.
Afterward, with your grace,
   may I be open to any evaluation,
   grateful for positive comments
   and gracious in accepting criticism,
   not defensive.
I rely on you to turn this stressful day
   into a pleasant memory. *Amen.*

Prayer before Speaking to Parents

Jesus, I am about to meet with my students' parents.
Give me the ears to listen to them
   and the words to support them.
Theirs is the challenging role
   of raising faithful Christians
   in a culture that often teaches
   the opposite of what you taught.

I don't know the burdens and troubles
   they are dealing with at home.
They may be facing financial problems,
   looking for a job,
     caring for an elderly parent or relative,
     or coping with a serious health issue.
Help me to encourage them.

Let me praise their children,
   pointing out their strengths
   and accomplishments.
May I tell the parents
   that I am happy that their child
   is in my class (if it is true).

When I must ask parents to help
   in curbing their children's misbehavior,
   let me do it with prudence and tact.
If they defend their child or criticize me,
   let me not argue but respond
   with gentleness and kindness.

Help me to make it clear
   that we are partners,
   and I will be glad to do
   what I can to assist them.
Remind me to assure them
of my prayers for their families. *Amen.*

Prayer for When I'm Assessing Students

Jesus, guide me in being honest and fair
   as I evaluate my students'
   progress and behavior.

May those high achievers
   be proud of themselves
   and keep up the good work.
May those whose performance
   leaves something to be desired
   be motivated to improve.

I hope I can tell from the students' actions
   that my teaching is making an impact

on them—that they are
kinder, more prayerful, and
more eager to learn about you.

I wonder how my students
would assess my teaching.
More important, I hope you are pleased
with how I teach in your name.
I would like to hear you say,
"Well done, good and faithful servant." *Amen.*

Prayer to Prepare for the Unexpected

Jesus, I never know what the future holds.
Any crisis can occur and disrupt
what I hope will be a flawless lesson.
A student may faint, have a nosebleed,
or storm out of the room.
An electrical outage could ruin
my PowerPoint or video.
A bee could fly in the window
and cause a commotion.
I could forget to bring part
of my lesson: a visual aid, a song,
or even the lesson plan!

No matter what happens,
give me the courage, stamina, and know-how
to deal with it calmly and successfully.
Let me be a good model for my students.

In the meantime, I will not worry
because I know that you are at my side
as I face any ordeal. *Amen.*

Prayer after a Tragedy

Jesus, when my students are overcome
by sorrow or fear because of a tragedy—
   like an illness, a divorce, a death,
   an accident, a fire, tornado, or flood—
     bring them peace.

Give me the words and actions
to soothe and comfort them
   in their distress.
May they turn to you
for the strength and courage
   to bear their cross.
Let them know that you are
   aware of their feelings
   and share their sorrow.
Instill in them the hope that
   tomorrow will be better
   and all will turn out for the good
   in your loving hands. *Amen.*

Prayer at the End of the School Year

Jesus, thank you for the privilege
   of teaching in your footsteps.
Thank you for my successes,
   known and unknown.
Forgive me for my failures.
   May I learn from them.

Bless my students during the summer.
May they enjoy playing with friends,
   being outside in nature,
   traveling or camping,
   and spending time with their families.
May they enrich their vacation
   by reading, working on a hobby,
   learning a musical instrument,
   or helping someone, like Mom or Dad.
Keep them safe from physical harm
   and from sin.
Help them to stay close to you
   by praying and going to Sunday Mass.
May they remember at least
   some of what I taught them!

Let me use my free weeks
   to perfect my teaching skills,
   learn more about my faith,
   and come to know you more intimately.
And let me not forget to relax, rest, and play
   in order to renew my energy.
Then I will be better prepared
   and more worthy to serve
   as your ambassador for another year. *Amen.*

PRAYERS TO
My Special Aides

Prayer to the Holy Spirit

Dear Holy Spirit,
set me on fire with zeal
 in leading my students
  to know and love God.
Call forth from me your gifts
 of wisdom, understanding, counsel,
 fortitude, knowledge, piety,
 and fear of the Lord.
All of these will help me succeed
 in carrying out my mission.

I believe that you live and act
 deep within me.
Be my invisible partner
 in the classroom.
Inspire me to teach generously,
 wholeheartedly, and effectively.
You empowered Jesus.
Now empower me
 as I strive to make your Church
 more alive
 by fostering the light of faith
 in my students. *Amen.*

Prayer to Mother Mary

Dear Mother of God and my mother,
  you were the first one to teach Jesus.
He learned to talk sitting on your lap
  and to walk holding your hands.
You taught him to pray
  and to practice the Jewish faith.
You were his first and best disciple.

I have said yes to God's call
  to teach in the name of your Son.
Pray for me that I live this yes
  as faithfully as you lived yours.

Help me to become a good catechist
  for those students God entrusts to me.
May they become devoted disciples of Jesus,
  bold and knowledgeable
    in speaking his Good News
  and faithful in walking his way.
And through me may they come to know
  that you are their loving
    heavenly mother. *Amen.*

Prayer to Saint Joseph

Saint Joseph, as the foster father of Jesus,
    you were his guardian and teacher.
He looked to you as a model
    for living as a man on Earth.
Besides raising him in the Jewish faith,
    you taught him the art of carpentry.
Pray that I serve as a model Christian
    for the students assigned to me,
    teaching them the art of loving God
        and their brothers and sisters.

As patron of the universal Church,
    you care for the mystical body of Jesus.
Ask God to give me the grace to form
    the young church members I teach
    into fervent Christians
    who have a close relationship with God.
May they be committed to building a better world
    and destined for heaven as their final home. *Amen.*

Prayer to Guardian Angels

Guardian Angels of my students,
    protect them from the devil's traps.
Keep them focused on their loving Father
    and his plans for their lives.
With your help, they will be formed into
    people of integrity and holiness.
Then someday they will be worthy
    to join you in heaven,
        praising our God forever.

And my dear Guardian Angel,
    guide me as I work to draw more people
    to the God whom we both love and adore.
Protect me from the temptations
    to do less than my best,
    to speak ill of my students,
    and to discipline harshly.
Make my efforts fruitful
    for the sake of the world
    and for the honor and glory of God. *Amen.*

Prayer to Saint Charles Borromeo

Saint Charles Borromeo,
patron saint of catechists,
    more than four hundred years ago
    you helped write the Roman catechism
    and established weekly religion classes
    in your diocese.
Today I am proud and honored
to be involved in the same great work
    of teaching God's word.

Pray for me that I reflect
    the wisdom and love needed to impart
    to my students the faith you professed.
May I always strive to carry out well
    my unique role in the Church.
Also pray for my students that they
    receive the Good News with joy
    and pass it on to others. *Amen.*

PRAYERS FOR Holidays, Holy Days, and Seasons

Prayer before the Feast of All Saints

Jesus, my students are excited
about their Halloween costumes
   and collecting bags of goodies.
I want them to be sure to know
that this holiday is the eve
of the feast of the hallowed ones,
   the saints, who are united
   with us in the Communion of Saints.

I would like to teach my students
   three facts:
We are all created to be saints.
The lives of the saints show us
   how to live as God wants.
The saints were human,
   and so had faults like us,
   but with God's grace
      they reached heaven.

Guide me in acquainting my students
with saints who will inspire them
   to live good lives themselves.
These may be popular saints
   like Saint Francis of Assisi
   and Saint Thérèse of Lisieux
as well as saints from the United States
   like Saint Kateri Tekakwitha
   and Saint John Neumann.

May I encourage my students
to think of the saints as friends
    who are willing to pray for them.
These include their patron saints
    and, of course, Saint Anthony,
    who helps locate lost things.

Let me not forget
to remind my students and their parents
    that All Saints Day is a day
    when we are required
    to celebrate the Eucharist.

I hope that someday the saints
will welcome me and all my students
    to their heavenly home. *Amen.*

Prayer before Thanksgiving

Jesus, you knew the value of saying thank you.
You thanked the Father for hearing your prayers.
And you thanked him before multiplying bread
    and before instituting the Eucharist.

As my students prepare to dine
on their Thanksgiving Day feast,
    despite any hardships they may endure
    let them remember to thank God
    for all the blessings they do enjoy,
        like their life, family, food,
        and all the wonders of the world.

Recalling God's many favors
    will lead them to worship.

It will also deepen their love
    for our good and provident God.

Help me to teach the importance
    of the virtue of thanksgiving.
I want to be a model of gratitude
    by inviting prayers of thanks during class
    and by being quick to thank my students
        whenever I have a chance.

I intend to explain to my students
that the word *Eucharist* means thanksgiving
    and that participating in Mass
    is the perfect way to thank God.
Thank YOU for that incredible gift! *Amen.*

Prayer before Advent

Jesus, as the lovely season of Advent nears,
    may I resolve to focus
        on your three wonderful comings.
As I eagerly prepare to celebrate
    your first coming at Christmas,
let me look forward with hope to
    your final coming at the end of the world
and be aware of your coming every day
    in other people, events, and the Eucharist.

Keep me from being so caught up
    in the frenzy of pre-Christmas
        shopping, decorating, and sending cards
    that I forget about you.
May I go about these tasks serenely,
    with my mind and heart centered on you.

I hope that my students and I await you
as your Blessed Mother did:
   with joyful anticipation
   and heartfelt gratitude. *Amen.*

Prayer before Christmas

Jesus, it astounds me that you,
   almighty God,
   came to Earth as a helpless baby.
You could have appeared
   as a full-grown prince in a palace.
Instead, you were born
   to a young peasant girl in a lowly shelter.

You are the Savior the world needed.
   Angels, shepherds, and kings rejoiced.
I, too, rejoice and am awed
   at the depth of God's love
   for us human creatures.

May my students remember
   the real meaning of Christmas.
You, Jesus, are the star of the day.
Keep Santa Claus and presents
   from upstaging the tremendous miracle
   of your appearance on Earth.

I will try hard to keep my students
   focused on you this Christmas.
I pray that they realize that the Christmas tree,
   tinsel, ornaments, candles, and wreaths
   are all in your honor.

May they sing Christmas carols about you
    along with songs about jingle bells and snow.
And may they and their families
    be at the Christmas Mass
    to celebrate and give thanks that
    in our darkness you,
    the Light of the World, came to us.

While we exchange Christmas gifts,
    I know that our best gift is you!
My gift in return is all I am and all my love. *Amen.*

Prayer at the New Year

Jesus, I am halfway
    through the school year.
It is a good time
    to assess my teaching so far
    and make new year's resolutions
    for future classes.

Please enlighten me
    to know how I can improve.
I want to do my best
    in drawing all the students
    closer to you.
Guide me in choosing
    the lessons they most need.
Inspire me with ways
to produce powerful, exciting lessons
    that they will remember.

As the weeks roll on,
keep my zeal for teaching
    fresh and strong, Jesus.

And help me to grow in the virtues
 of an excellent catechist:
 faith, hope, and love,
 as well as wisdom and patience. *Amen.*

Prayer before Lent

Jesus, the grace-filled season of Lent
 is my time for renewal
 and spiritual growth.
During these weeks, help me
to breathe new life into my daily prayers,
 increase my almsgiving,
 and practice fasting
  not only from food
  but from bad habits.

I wish to spend these days
 reflecting on your terrible passion and death
  that redeemed me with all humankind,
 realizing anew the depths
 of your love for me.

As I meet with my students during Lent,
may I convey how your love for them
 evoked your mercy and forgiveness.
May I encourage them
to think of practical resolutions
 that will make them better Christians
 and strengthen their relationship with you,
 our crucified and resurrected Savior. *Amen.*

Prayer before Easter

Jesus, help me to impress
on my students that Easter
   is the greatest feast of all:
   greater than Christmas.
I want them to understand
that your rising from the dead
   means resurrection
   and eternal life for us.
Besides, it is the foundation
   of our faith.

My students will be dyeing eggs
and anticipating receiving baskets
   filled with all kinds of candy.
May they realize
that the reason for their celebration
   is your victory over sin and death,
   a gift far sweeter than chocolate!
In you, life has overcome death.
Good has triumphed over evil.

May my students' families participate
in the beautiful church services
   of the Easter Triduum.
I look forward to being with them,
   singing, "Alleluia, praise God!"
   with all my heart.
With the help of your grace,
we will celebrate Easter forever
   in your kingdom,
rejoicing with countless angels and saints
and praising you face to face. *Amen.*